# Contents

Dead Famous! .............................................. 2

Room 1: What on Earth is a Dinosaur? ........ 4

Room 2: The Fossil Room ............................ 8

Room 3: The Dinosaur Room ...................... 20

Room 4: Dinosaur Bloopers! ....................... 30

Room 5: End of the Dinosaurs .................... 34

Glossary .................................................... 38

Index .......................................................... 39

# Dead Famous!

Dinosaurs are *really* famous. Their name means 'terrible lizard'. We see them in movies. We read about them in books and magazines. There are even dinosaur action figures and cuddly toys. This is pretty impressive, especially when you think that the last land-living dinosaurs died out 66 million years ago.

Meet Jamal. He loves dinosaurs.

This is Sally. She's a **palaeontologist**, and she's a dinosaur expert.

Hi!

Hello!

Everyone knows something about dinosaurs, but even scientists like Sally don't know everything, and sometimes, they get things wrong. New dinosaurs are discovered every few weeks, and scientists are always learning something new.

If we want to find out about lions or monkeys, we can study them in the wild, or see them in a zoo. But finding out about **prehistoric** dinosaurs isn't so easy.

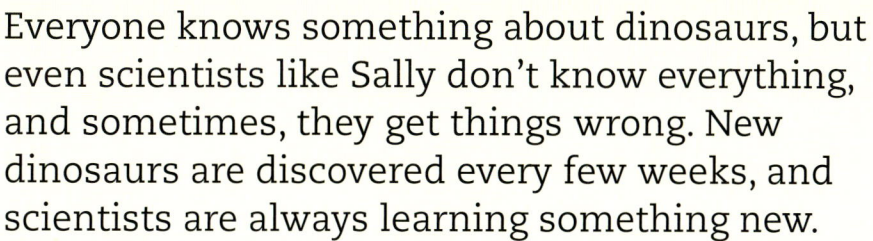

So, how do we find out about them?

We need to hunt for them. But first, we have to know what we're hunting for. Come into the museum. All the answers we need are in here.

# Room 1: What on Earth is a Dinosaur?

Prehistoric dinosaurs ruled the land for around 152 million years. They lived during the Mesozoic era, between 66 and 252 million years ago.

The Mesozoic era is divided into three time periods: the Triassic, the Jurassic, and the Cretaceous.

Sometimes, people call the Triassic the 'Age of Reptiles'.

The deeper down something is, the older it is.

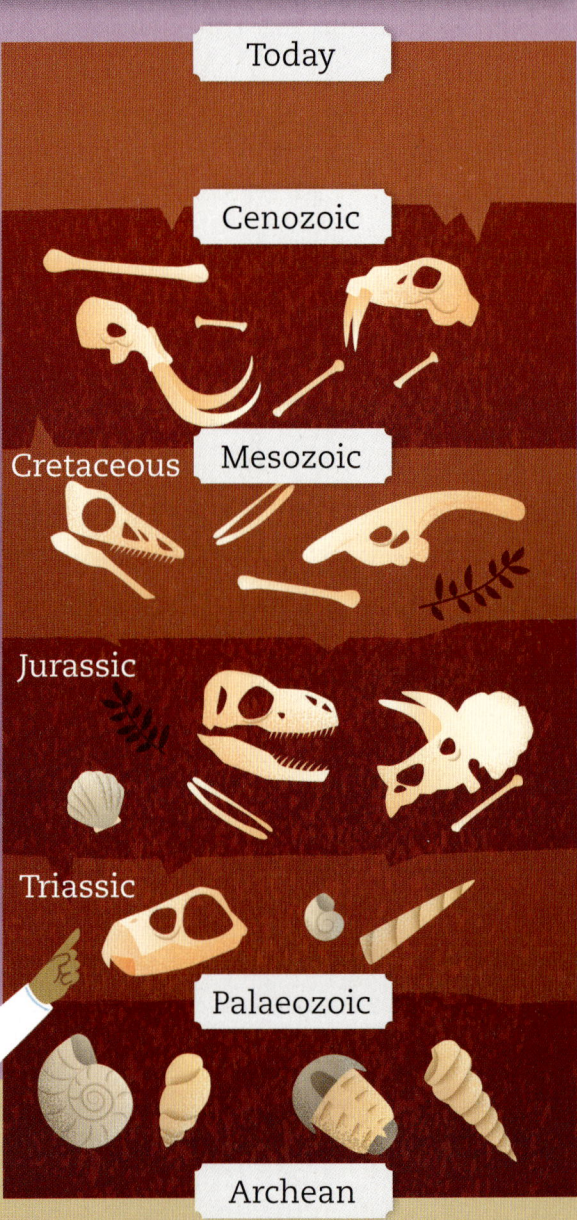

4

Like lizards today, prehistoric dinosaurs were reptiles. Although dinosaurs have things in common with other reptiles, there is one important thing that makes them different. Dinosaurs could stand with their back legs straight, underneath their bodies.

This meant that dinosaurs could easily support their own weight and use less energy when they moved around. It also meant they could run faster than other reptiles.

Other reptile legs

Dinosaur legs

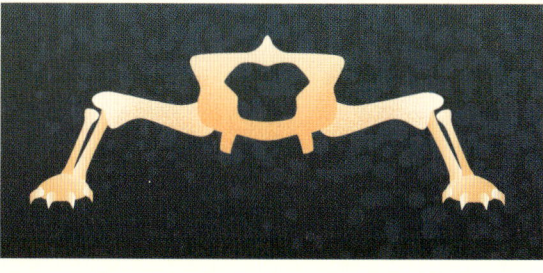
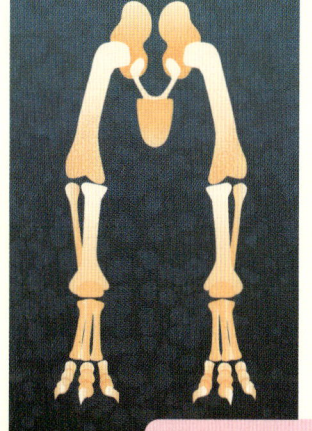

This difference might not seem much to you, but it's very useful for scientists. It makes it easier to see if what they have discovered is a dinosaur or not.

Some things that people think are dinosaurs, are not actually dinosaurs at all. Let's go and see some of them.

# Not dinosaurs

There were lots of other prehistoric creatures, and it's easy to mix them up with dinosaurs, but there are some important differences!

### In the sky

**NOT DINOSAURS!**

Pterodactyls (say: *tera-dak-tils*) and Quetzalcoatlus (say: *quet-zal-coat-lus*) are pterosaurs (say: *tera-saws*). Pterosaurs are an extinct group of flying reptile. Their wings were made of skin that stretched over a very long fourth finger.

Pterosaur wing

Quetzalcoatlus are the largest known flying creatures to have existed. When on the ground, they would have stood as tall as a giraffe.

Quetzalcoatlus   Giraffe

## Under the sea  **NOT DINOSAURS!**

Mosasaurs (say: *mow-zuh-saws*), plesiosaurs (say: *plee-see-oh-saurs*) and ichthyosaurs (say: *ik-thee-oh-saurs*) lived in the sea.

These sea creatures also gave birth to live young, while dinosaurs laid eggs.

## On the Land  **NOT DINOSAURS!**

Dinosaurs lived on the land. But not every prehistoric land creature was a dinosaur. Dimetrodons (say: *die-metro-dons*) might look like dinosaurs, but they died out 40 million years before the first dinosaurs ever lived. Just take a look at their legs – they stick out like a crocodile's, so they can't be dinosaurs.

Mosasaur

Plesiosaur

Ichthyosaur

Dimetrodon

If dinosaurs lived so long ago, how do we even know about them?

That's a good question. Come with me and I'll show you.

# Room 2: The Fossil Room

Wow! Look at those bones!

Fossilised dinosaur bones

Fossils aren't actual bones, they're rocks.

Everything we know about dinosaurs comes from fossils. When a plant or an animal dies, the remains normally rot away, leaving nothing behind. For something to become a fossil, the conditions must be just right.

First, the remains have to be quickly buried by a layer of **sediment**. This is often mud or sand from a river. This layer helps protect the remains from the weather *and* other creatures.

After a while, usually only the hard parts of the creature are left – bones, teeth, horns and claws. More layers build up, squashing the sediment and turning it into rock.

This is called **'sedimentary rock'**.

This process is called fossilisation.

Water seeps in and gradually wears away the remains. **Minerals** in the water replace the remains, leaving behind a perfect rock copy – a fossil.

Things that die today could become fossils, but it takes at least 10,000 years. The most recent fossils are from Woolly mammoths, which appeared on Earth around 300,000 years ago, 65 million years after the dinosaurs.

Woolly mammoth

# What fossils can tell us

We know what dinosaurs looked like because fossils give palaeontologists clues. Fossils aren't usually of a complete dinosaur. Often, there are only a few pieces, so palaeontologists have to work out what kind of dinosaur they're from.

They do this by comparing new finds with fossils that were found in the past. They also compare them with creatures living today.

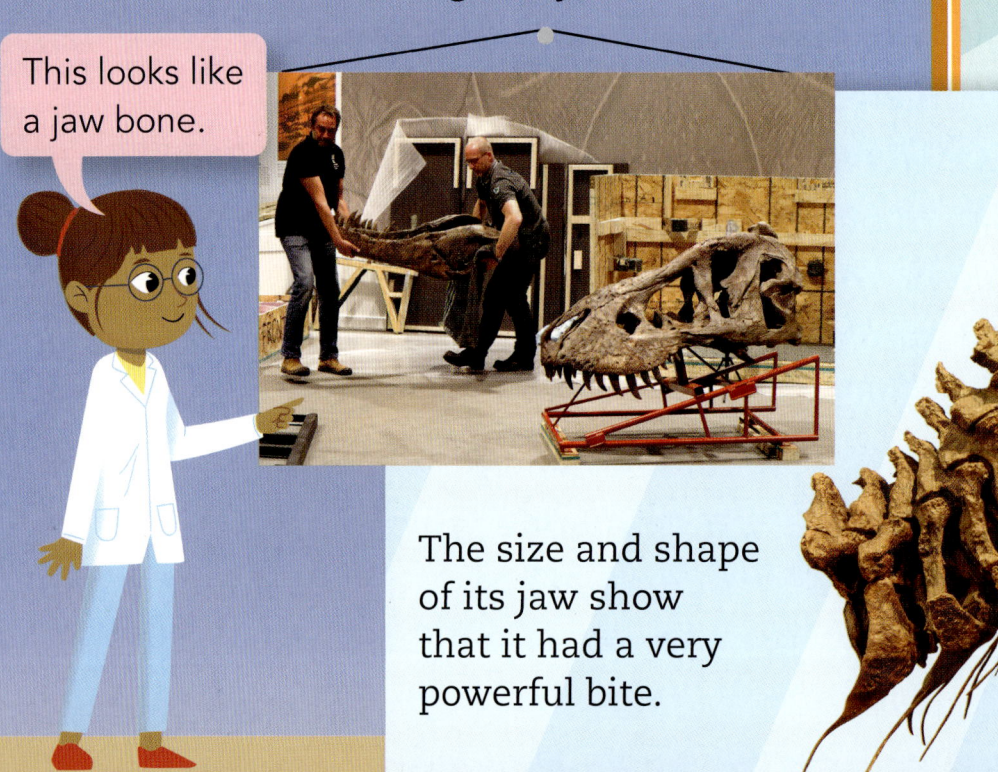

This looks like a jaw bone.

The size and shape of its jaw show that it had a very powerful bite.

The large eyes suggest that the T Rex had very good eyesight. There's enough space in the skull for quite a large brain, which tells us that it was an intelligent creature – probably as clever as a chimpanzee.

Fossils of bones, teeth, horns and claws are called body fossils. But other types of fossils can be found too, and they can tell us interesting things.

The sharp pointed teeth of this Tyrannosaurus tell us it was a **carnivore**.

This looks like it was a fearsome predator.

Let's go and see some other fossils.

Tyrannosaurus skull

## Trace fossils

Trace fossils are fossils that show traces of where a dinosaur was, or what it was doing. These include things like footprints, eggshells, **dung** and marks left by skin or feathers.

We can find out what the dinosaur has been eating by examining coprolites.

Pieces of fossilised dung are called coprolites.

Coprolites

Wow! Fossilised footprints!

## Ichnites

Fossilised footprints are called ichnites (say: *ik-nights*). They can tell us about the way dinosaurs moved around. By looking at them, scientists can see that some dinosaurs moved in groups or herds.

The way the prints are spaced can show if the dinosaur was running. Scientists even use prints to help work out how quickly a dinosaur could walk.

In 2021, a four-year-old girl discovered a footprint on a beach in Wales. Scientists compared the print with other fossils and worked out that it might have been made by a small **herbivore**, 200 million years ago.

You don't have to be a palaeontologist to find an interesting fossil.

So where can you find fossils?

Let's go and see.

## Finding fossils

To learn about dinosaurs, scientists need to study fossils, but finding them isn't always easy. Because fossils are created underground, most of them are buried deep beneath the surface. The deeper a fossil is buried, the older it is. To find fossils, palaeontologists must dig down, or wait for the fossils to come to the surface.

## Digging down

Lots of fossils have been discovered by miners who were looking for other valuable things, like gold, silver, diamonds and coal.

In 2011, miners in Alberta, Canada, discovered the fossilised remains of a nodosaur (say: *no-doh-saur*).

It was so well preserved that scientists could tell what it had been eating.

Nodosaur

## Coming to the surface

Fossils can come to the surface when the ground they are in gets pushed upwards by movements in the Earth. They can also come to the surface if the ground covering them gets worn away by the sea or weather. Cliffs are a great place for fossil hunters.

In 2020, walkers on the Isle of Wight found the fossilised tail of an Iguanodon.

Iguanodon tail fossil

Nodosaur fossil

# What's in a name?

Dinosaurs are usually named by the people that discover them. Their names sometimes tell us what type of dinosaur they are. Names can also show where they were found and who found them.

Could a dinosaur be called Bob?

That couldn't be its proper name because there are rules for naming living or extinct **organisms**.

The name must be in two parts, like Tyrannosaurus rex.

'Tyrannosaurus' is the **genus** name, and 'rex' is the **species** name.

This means there's a specific tyrannosaur called Tyrannosaurus rex.

Most people only use the first part of a dinosaur's name, like Triceratops (say: *tri-cer-ra-tops*). We wouldn't normally say Triceratops horridus, or Triceratops prorsus.

Triceratops

Here are some words used in dinosaur names. Can you work out what Tyrannosaurus rex means?

allo – strange

bronto – thunder

cerat – horned

compso – pretty

draco – dragon

don – tooth

echino – spiked

elasmo – plated

nodo – lumpy

onyx – claw

ops – face

raptor – robber

rex – king

saurus – lizard

stego – roof

tyranno – tyrant

Make up your own dinosaur name! It can be silly or sensible.

Most words palaeontologists use come from Latin or ancient Greek, because these were the languages of science.

# Star Fossil Hunters

## Mary Anning

Mary was born in England in 1799. She hunted for fossils on Lyme Regis beach and made her living by selling them to visitors. She made many important discoveries. When she was only 12, Mary discovered the first known Ichthyosaurus.

Mary Anning

At that time, women weren't encouraged to do science, so Mary didn't receive the recognition she deserved. However, today she's recognised as one of the most important figures in palaeontology.

Icthyosaurus fossil

# Roy Chapman Andrews

Roy Chapman Andrews was born in the USA in 1884, and led expeditions into the Gobi Desert and Mongolia. Because of his work, we know that dinosaurs laid eggs. He discovered the first known dinosaur eggs, belonging to an Oviraptor (say: *oh-ve-rap-tor*). He was the inspiration for the movie hero, Indiana Jones.

Roy Chapman Andrews

Oviraptor

Indiana Jones

# Xu Xing

Xu Xing (say: *Shoo Shing*) was born in China in 1969. He has discovered and named more dinosaurs than any other palaeontologist in the world, including the Microraptor.*

His discoveries have revealed that many dinosaurs had feathers.

Xu Xing

Microraptor fossil

*Read more about Microraptors on page 27.

# Room 3: The Dinosaur Room

In this room are some different types of dinosaurs that we've discovered.

To help identify dinosaurs, palaeontologists group together those with similar features.

Sauropods, like Diplodocus, had large flat teeth, like cows have. This feature tells us they were herbivores. Their long necks suggest they probably ate leaves from tree tops.

Just like giraffes!

Diplodocus

Theropods, like Velociraptors, had the sharp pointed teeth of carnivores. By comparing therapods with living creatures, palaeontologists have worked out they walked upright on their back legs.

Velociraptor

T Rex and chicken skeletons are similar, but different sizes!

T Rex

chicken

Ceratopsians, like Triceratops, were herbivores with parrot-like beaks and bony frills. They often had horns, like the Anchiceratops (say: *an-key-serra-tops*).

Anchiceratops

Ornithopods, like Iguanodon, were three-toed herbivores. Early ornithopods were small and walked on two legs, but later ornithopods were huge and walked on four legs.

Iguanodon

Stegosaurus

Armoured dinosaurs, like Stegosaurus, were herbivores that walked on four legs. They often had spiked tails.

Pachycephalosaurus

Pachycephalosaurs (say: *pack-i-kef-al-oh-sores*), were herbivores that walked on two legs and had very thick skulls, like Pachycephalosaurus (say: *pack-i-kef-al-oh-sore-us*).

Palaeontologists think they might have butted heads – like some goats do. If they did, the thick skull would have protected their brain.

# Giants

Spinosaurus was even bigger than Tyrannosaurus rex. It's the largest carnivorous dinosaur we know of. Its head and teeth are like a crocodile's. We know from fossils that it ate fish, other dinosaurs and even flying pterosaurs.

Here are two giants of the dinosaur age: Spinosaurus (say: *spine-oh-sore-us*) and Argentinosaurus (say: *ar-jen-tee-no-sore-us*). We know much more about one than we do about the other.

In 1984, a smaller spinosaur, called a Baryonyx, was found in England.

Fish scales and Iguanodon bones were found inside it.

Spinosaurus

Spinosaurs are thought to be the only dinosaurs that could swim and hunt in water. Palaeontologists have worked this out from what they ate, where they've been found, and their head shape.

Spinosaurs have one extra-long claw, which they might have used to hook fish.

Guess what? Some bears still do that today!

## Argentinosaurus

Argentinosaurus is the biggest land-living creature to have been found.

Scientists think it could have been 35 metres long – about the same length as three buses! But only a few pieces have been found, so no one is really sure.

Argentinosaurus

# Tiny terrors

Shuvuuia (say: *shu-voo-ee-ah*) is Mongolian for 'bird'. The chicken-sized Shuvuuia lived in the desert in Mongolia, and probably used their sharp claws to dig into **termite** mounds for food. We know there were termites where the Shuvuuia lived, and today, animals like aardvarks and anteaters use their claws to do the same thing. Shuvuuia's very large eyes and ears tell us that they probably hunted in the dark, like owls.

Were all dinosaurs big?

No! Some were very small.

Shuvuuia

Microraptor

4 wings

30 cm

Microraptor (which means tiny grabber), was a four-winged dinosaur. Palaeontologists think its muscles weren't strong enough for flying.

Fossilised Microraptors have been found with their last meals still inside them. From this, we know they ate fish, lizards, small mammals and birds.

Bones and teeth can't tell us about the colour of a dinosaur, but feathers are different. By carefully examining fossilised feathers, and comparing them with different coloured feathers of birds living today, scientists have been able to tell that Microraptor feathers were glossy and black.

But those wings would have been perfect for gliding from tree to tree.

These little dinosaurs are cool, but I'd like to see a T Rex.

Come on, there are some tyrannosaurs over here!

# Tyrannosaurs

There are about 30 different species of tyrannosaur, but not all of them were big like Tyrannosaurus rex.

## Small

One of the earliest known tyrannosaurs is the Guanlong (say: *gwan-long*), meaning 'crowned dragon'. Guanlong lived in China during the late Jurassic period. It was small with very sharp teeth.

> Those sharp teeth show it was a carnivore, so you wouldn't want one chasing you!

Guanlong had a crest on their heads. Palaeontologists think their bodies probably had a coat of feathers or fine hairs, because they have found similar tyrannosaurs with signs of fossilised feathers or hairs.

Guanlong

Eotyrannus

## Medium

Eotyrannus (which means 'early tyrant'), lived during the early Cretaceous period. Fossils of Eotyrannus were found on the Isle of Wight.

## Large

Yutyrannus lived during the early Cretaceous period and was found in China. This large relative died out over 50 million years before the first Tyrannosaurus rex walked the Earth.

## Rex

Tyrannosaurus rex lived during the late Cretaceous period, between 68 and 66 million years ago. It was the biggest of the tyrannosaurs. The largest one ever found was 12.6 metres long.

Yutyrannus

Tyrannosaurus rex

# Room 4: Dinosaur Bloopers!

Welcome to the bloopers room! Here we'll find out about some of the mistakes people have made about dinosaurs.

Why do you think people might have got things wrong?

1. It's very hard to study something that's been dead for millions of years.
2. Palaeontologists don't always agree with each other.
3. Most fossilised remains are incomplete, so it's not always easy to know which dinosaur a fossil belongs to.
4. Early dinosaur hunters weren't always as careful as they are today.
5. Beneath the ground, fossils can be squashed out of shape, too.

"Some palaeontologists used dynamite to uncover fossils."

Luckily, improvements in technology have helped palaeontologists to make new discoveries and learn more.

Richard Owen

The palaeontologist Richard Owen chose the name 'dinosaur' – meaning 'terrible lizard' – back in 1841. Because of this, people thought that dinosaurs must all have had scales like lizards.

**Wrong!**

Palaeontologists now know that some dinosaurs had fur or feathers, especially theropods. Remains of a Yutyrannus showed that it was covered in fur for warmth.

hair

Yutyrannus

## Loud roars

In movies, most dinosaurs roar to make them seem more frightening. Palaeontologists today don't think that dinosaurs would have made noises like this at all.

By examining fossilised remains and comparing them to things living today, scientists have worked out that some dinosaurs would make deep, low sounds, like crocodiles. Others probably made sounds like birds.

A lot of people get their dinosaur knowledge from movies, but the details aren't always correct.

Today, predators like lions hunt silently. Roaring would scare their prey away.

## Dinosaur rumble

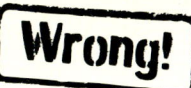

Dinosaurs like Tyrannosaurus rex and Stegosaurus are often shown fighting each other in movies. This could never have happened. Stegosaurus had been extinct for millions of years before Tyrannosaurus rex walked the Earth. They were already fossils beneath the ground.

> We live closer in time to Tyrannosaurus rex than Stegosaurus did.

170  150  130  110  90  70  50  30  10  now
**millions of years ago**

People often think all dinosaurs roamed the Earth at the same time. But we now know that some dinosaurs would never have even met.

# Room 5: End of the Dinosaurs

From the fossils that have been found, we know that prehistoric dinosaurs roamed the Earth for over 170 million years. In that time, they changed and **evolved**. Some died out and new ones came along. But then something happened that wiped out all the land-living dinosaurs.

What was it?

It's believed that this **mass extinction** was partly caused by the effects of a huge **asteroid** hitting Mexico, in what is now called the Yucatán Peninsula, and partly by huge volcanoes erupting in India at the same time.

The effects of the asteroid collision were terrible. It created an enormous cloud of dust and soot that spread across the world. This cloud **suffocated** many creatures, and stopped warmth and light from the Sun from getting through.

Without sunlight, plants soon died out, leaving very little for the remaining creatures to eat.

It's thought that around three-quarters of life on Earth came to an end.

But not all dinosaurs died out …

The asteroid made a crater 150 km wide.

That's wider than 1600 football pitches!

# Survivors

The birds we see today are actually living dinosaurs. They are the direct descendants of therapods. Some birds even look like prehistoric dinosaurs.

Cassowary

Just look at this cassowary, from Australia.

It reminds me of a citipati.

Citipati is an **oviraptorid** dinosaur that lived in the late Cretaceous period, between 81 and 75 million years ago. This **omnivore** didn't have teeth, so it probably pecked fruit and small animals with its beak – just like the cassowary does today.

Citipati

Other creatures, like crocodiles, alligators, snakes and lizards are closely related to dinosaurs too.

Even though the reign of the land-living dinosaur came to an end 66 million years ago, there is still a lot that we don't know about them. And the answers to our questions about them are lying beneath our feet.

Remember, you don't have to be a scientist to discover dinosaurs.

Next time you're out walking on the beach – keep your eyes open. You never know what you'll find.

You could be the next Mary Anning!

# Glossary

| | |
|---|---|
| **asteroid** | a large rock in space that orbits the sun |
| **carnivore** | a creature that eats meat |
| **dung** | animal droppings or waste |
| **evolved** | changed over a period of time |
| **genus** | a group of living things that are similar, and closely related to each other |
| **herbivore** | a creature that eats plants |
| **mass extinction** | a lot of creatures becoming extinct at the same time |
| **minerals** | hard substances that occur naturally in the ground and in rocks |
| **omnivore** | a creature that eats a mixture of meat and plants |
| **organisms** | an individual animal, plant or single-cell life form |
| **oviraptorid** | a type of dinosaur with a toothless beak, a claw and a crest on its skull |
| **palaeontologist** | a scientist who studies fossils and dinosaurs |
| **prehistoric** | the time in history before things were written down and recorded |
| **sediment** | small pieces of solid material, like sand, that sink to the bottom of water |
| **sedimentary rock** | rock that has been created by the build-up of sediment |
| **species** | a particular type of living thing |
| **suffocated** | to have died due to a lack of oxygen |
| **termite** | an insect similar to an ant |

# Index

armoured dinosaurs  23

asteroid  34–35, 38

carnivore  11, 21, 28, 38

ceratopsians  22

coprolites  12

Cretaceous  4, 29, 36

dinosaur legs  5, 7, 21, 22, 23

extinct(ion)  6, 16, 33, 34

fossil  8–15, 18, 19, 24, 27–34

herbivore  13, 20, 22–23, 38

ichnites  13

Isle of Wight  15, 29

Jurassic  4, 28

Mary Anning  18, 37

omnivore  36, 38

ornithopods  22

oviraptorid  36, 38

pachycephalosaurs  23

palaeontologist  2, 10, 13, 14, 17, 18–19, 20–21, 23, 25, 27, 28, 30–32, 38

prehistoric  3, 4, 5, 6, 7, 34, 36, 38

pterosaurs  6, 24

Richard Owen  31

Roy Chapman Andrews  19

sauropods  20

sedimentary rock  9, 38

theropods  21, 31

Triassic  4

tyrannosaurs  27–29

Tyrannosaurus rex (T Rex)  11, 16–17, 21, 24, 27, 28–29, 33, 40

Xu Xing  19

# Now answer the questions ...

1. What does a palaeontologist do?
2. What is an 'era'?
3. Look at page 11. What word does the author use to show that palaeontologists can't be absolutely sure how intelligent a T Rex was?
4. Look at the photo of the cliff at the top of page 15. What might happen here after a storm?
5. Work out what the name *Triceratops* means.
6. Look at the diagrams on page 29. Why does the author include the silhouette of a person next to the dinosaurs?
7. Look at page 31. How might dynamite have caused problems for fossil hunters?
8. Why do movies about dinosaurs sometimes include incorrect details about them?
9. What in the world today shows that not all dinosaurs were wiped out by the asteroid collision?
10. Which dinosaur would you most and least like to meet? Why?

# A note from the author

I've always been fascinated with dinosaurs and how we know about these creatures that lived so long ago. When I was 12 years old, we walked on the beach near some cliffs and left footprints in the sand that showed we had been there. There, amongst the rocks and shells, we found fossils – traces of creatures that had been in that same place millions of years ago and left their own prints behind.

## Now try this!

Write a news report that describes the discovery of an interesting fossil in your area.

A dinosaur found by a girl called Daisy Morris was given the name *Vectidraco daisymorrisae* (Vecti means Isle of Wight). Use the naming words on page 17 to help you make up a dinosaur named after you!

Look out for fossils in your area. Can you spot any in marble worktops, stone paving slabs, among pebbles, or on buildings as decorations?

Make a model or draw a picture of a newly discovered dinosaur. What will it look like? Will it have fur or wings or sharp teeth or spines on its back? Give it a name!

**Cosmos**

Dinosaurs are *really* famous. We see them in movies. We read about them in books and magazines. There are even dinosaur action figures and cuddly toys. This is pretty impressive, especially when you think that the last land-living dinosaurs died out 66 million years ago!

This book will take you on a visit to the dinosaur museum, where you'll discover:

- the ways that dinosaurs are classified and what their names mean
- how people identify dinosaurs from their fossils
- the mistakes people have made about dinosaurs
- what happened to the dinosaurs and whether they still exist today …

Also available:

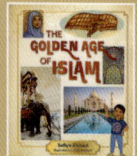
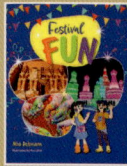

VENUS / Brown B

ISBN 978-1-3983-7726-4

9 781398 377264

www.hoddereducation.com